The Challenges of the Church in the 21st Century

Larry Musa Ndlovu

Order this book online at www.trafford.com
or email orders@trafford.com

Most Trafford titles are also available at major online book retailers.

Printed in Victoria, BC, Canada.

ISBN: 978-1-4251-9025-5

Our mission is to efficiently provide the world's finest, most comprehensive book publishing service, enabling every author to experience success. To find out how to publish your book, your way, and have it available worldwide, visit us online at www.trafford.com

Trafford rev. 1/19/2010

Trafford®
PUBLISHING www.trafford.com

North America & international
toll-free: 1 888 232 4444 (USA & Canada)
phone: 250 383 6864 ♦ fax: 812 355 4082

Dedication

To my lovely wife Nkosazana and my handsome son Judah, and to your future generation. You are my source of love, support, strength and motivation. My greatest FAMILY.

Contents

Preface

I forever remain challenged by the profound pre and fro up to date of this context. God has certainly poured out from heaven or emptied Himself in a volume, this book, which can be difficult to fathom without spiritual direction and leadership through the Holy Spirit. This work is purely for the purpose of guiding and leading His Church whilst on earth.

The purpose of this book addresses current challenges facing the 21st Century Church. The main challenges facing the church in this century are DECEPTION and MATERIALISM, through these elements the devil is drawing many away from the heavenly calling using FALSE SHEPHERDS, who preach carnally twisted and self enticing messages.

As you read through this book, you will discover how the devil is stripped off his tricks and exposed to shame; how God purposely reveals Himself to restore His CHURCH back to HER original GLORY.

SPIRITUAL DISCERNMENT is the key to spotting false shepherds and their schemes. My prayer is that by the Spirit of God you may gain understanding that will empower and inspire your walk with God.

Finally, it is that you may discover your TRUE GOD and your FINAL SPIRITUAL DESTINY.

Acknowledgments

Firstly, I want to acknowledge the Holy Spirit of God who has been an inspiring technology and a divine source of guidance and leadership during the writing of this book.

I want to thank all the people at Trafford Publishing, who have given much support to me with my first book and they have done such a fine job on it.

To Thoko Judah Mhlambo, thank you so much with all the editing, proofing and putting the book together. I want to say continue to shine Daughter of Zion. You were raised by God for such a time as this. Shine your light for the Nations to see glory of Jesus Christ.

Introduction

The Church is yet again at a place where she needs to be carefully redefined to effectively transition into the next level of the purposes of God whilst on earth. This is a spiritual must re-defining the process for the Church so that she stays relevant in the 21st Century.

The Church is entering a new critical hour in the spirit. This is that season where the church needs to undergo heavenly–leadership and structural adjustments; to be fully capacitated with all the spiritual gifting. She will be in the position to perform her end-time great exploits and fulfil the prophetic declaration as encountered in the Holy Scriptures. God is therefore placing a heavenly demand upon the Church leadership, the Shepherds, to conduct a self-audit through which will emerge a leadership that will reveal the sheep's knowledge of God. Her level of maturity and her ability to execute spiritual activities will then become clear.

There's an unavoidable mountain call for God's servants, the Shepherd of the Flock, to give an account in terms of the progress made thus far, and the quality of the work rendered for and on behalf of God. God is doing a spiritual audit of His House, the Church, so that the judgment process may be activated.

There is a serious concern about the quality of the Sheep (end-time harvest) produced and her condition thereof. For too long the Church has been caught up in growing up membership than producing a quality army of Christians. God can accomplish much with just a few that are genuinely baptized in the word than millions that do not even have a living relationship with Him.

Real Church is not the size and the architectural structure of buildings; it is the people; the human temple that is expected to worship God in spirit and in truth. The Church needs to abandon her old stronghold mentalities regarding the definition of her real identity. She needs to define herself in the context of God's make up and spiritual activity.

> *Haggai 1:2*
> *This is what the Lord Almighty says: "these people say, the time has not yet come for the Lord's house to be built". Then the word of the Lord came through the prophet Haggai: "is it a time for you yourselves to be living in your panelled houses while this house remains a ruin?"*

God expresses His deep concern regarding the current condition and the genuine spiritual identification of the Church. God defines the Church as His chosen people. It is not structures that are built and established by man's intellectual wisdom. In this passage of scripture the real house of God suffered a great deal of neglect, purely because people's priorities were self absorbing than God focused. At the unveiling of the process of the crucifixion Jesus said that He would destroy 'this' Temple (referring to His body) and build it up after three days.

God's priority right now is building and giving capacity to His Church so that she can be victorious in the end-time. God certainly wants to strengthen and empower us, so that we can face and overcome all earthly challenges imposed upon us by the enemy. There's an explosive power invested right within the Church into which we need must tap. Until the Church learns to operate in this anointing, she will remain limping and powerless to wrestle against spiritual forces and powers of darkness, much less winning earthly kingdoms for the Glory of our God.

God is demanding the Church to shift her focus from such evil and carnal inclinations, which will ultimately result in her destruction and damnation. The Church has to start focusing on spiritual values that can culminate in her victorious earthly lifestyle. Right now God is positioning His Church such that she can be able to translate into an immortal man through the life of the spirit.

The primary mandate of God's servants, the Shepherds, should be to feed and strengthen the sheep. They must never create false expectations for the sheep such as wanting to become rich through the kingdom by claiming certain breakthrough scriptures. The sheep is justifiably going through the motions of becoming rich some day; the church is therefore caught up in material possession than being possessed with God.

The sheep's focus is totally lost right now the church is no longer worshiping God in spirit and in truth as demanded. The act of coming before God, humbly kneel at His feet seeking His face and fulfil spiritual hunger is slowly diminishing. God is no longer God because He is God, but God is defined as God on the basis of material things that can be retrieved via prayer through Him. The sheep is clearly deceived, and therefore, needs to cry out loud to the Shepherd for restoration of truth.

Beyond a shadow of doubt there are many false shepherds out there operating in disguise and using the name of God in vain, for self enrichment at the expense of the sheep. God is extremely unhappy and deeply concerned about these false shepherds. This kingdom plunder is a cycling event that once upon a time happened in the Old Testament. The Church needs to fast and pray to God, so that He can release a relevant anointing to break it down.

It is for this reason that this book is inspired to exist. Thus, prayerfully allow God as you read through this book to give you a sense of spiritual understanding. And my prayer is that:

> *... out of his glorious riches he may strengthen you with power through his spirit in your inner being, so that Christ may dwell in your hearts through faith. And I pray that you, being rooted and established in love, may have power together with all the saints, to grasp how wide and long and high and deep is the love of Christ, and to know this love that surpasses knowledge that you may be filled to the measure of fullness of God.*
>
> *Ephesians 3:16-19*

Chapter 1

False Shepherds

Ezekiel 34

In this chapter, shepherds refer to leaders in the Church, pastors or those entrusted with the responsibility of looking after the sheep, the people of God. In this particular instance in Ezekiel 34, God is dealing with the shepherds who portrayed negligence and lack of care in conduct of their responsibility. It led to the scattering of the flock over the mountains of the nations. So God sends instruction through His servant the prophet, Ezekiel, to Israel's shepherds who have misrepresented Him to His people.

We need to note that the sheep is God's greatest asset that will forever have precious value in His sight. He bought them with His Son's special blood at the cross of Calvary. When God addresses the shepherds, He singles out the following areas as of significant concern.

Shepherds who only took care of themselves

This means that they were very self-centred; they never saw beyond the boundaries of self-fullness. What

1

mattered to them the most in this instance was self-image, wealth, health, finances, social state of affairs than shepherding the flock. Such a lifestyle was not true reflection of God's love to His flock. The shepherds only took care of themselves, failing in executing
the task entrusted to them by God.

We need to understand that both sheep and shepherd are equally important before God. However, the shepherds have a greater responsibility with which they are entrusted. When God calls us to a shepherding position, He expects us, shepherds, to execute the task on His behalf the way He would if He were to do it Himself. Therefore, it's really an honour to us to be entrusted with such an awesome responsibility.

When God calls us He expects us shepherds to execute the task on His behalf the way He would if He did Himself.

It's upon the shepherd to realize that God, in His absolute divine nature, can do everything alone without our help. But, because He loves us so much, He wants us to resemble Him in everything we do. When God appoints a shepherd over the flock, He is indirectly placing that individual in His position of leadership but on a lower scale. As we lead God's people, we need to remember that He is watching over both the leader and the flock and pays equal attention to both whenever they pray towards Him. In chapter 34 the failure of the shepherds to take care of the flock reached out to God, and caused Him to be very concerned.

Shepherds must realize that as we look after His flock, He on the other side takes care of our needs. A good shepherd dies to self and places on his priority list the life of the flock first. He seeks the best for the flock, identifies greener pastures, new opportunities, virgin grazing land, safe areas, always places his own life at risk by providing protection for the flock when the enemy or beast come to steal and destroy the flock.

Shepherds must always bear in mind that the flock is God's greatest asset. He bought us all with a special prize, by sending His only begotten Son, Jesus Christ to die for us all. Shepherds who ill-treat God's flock are false and never were appointed by God to look after His possession. We need to pray to God to remove them from such positions of leadership.

We need to remember that He is watching over both the leader and the flock with equal attention to both

The challenge is upon us as shepherds to copy from Jesus Christ and lead in the same way He lead God's people, subsequently obtaining favour from God. It is the responsibility of the Shepherd to look after the flock and it is God's business to look after the needs of the shepherd.

How to Identify False Shepherds
John 10:1-13

"I tell you truth, the man who does not enter the sheep by the gate, but climbs in by some other way, is a thief and a robber. The man who enters by the gate is the shepherd of his sheep. The watchman opens the gate for him, and the sheep listen to his voice. He calls

his own sheep by name and leads them out. When he has brought out all his own, he goes on ahead of them, and his sheep follow him because they know his voice. But they will never follow a stranger; in fact, they will run away from him because they do not recognize a stranger's voice."

Therefore Jesus said again, "I tell you the truth, I am the gate for the sheep. All who ever came before me were thieves and robbers, but the sheep did not listen to them. I am the gate; whoever enters through me will be saved. He will come in and go out, and find pasture. The thief comes only to steal and kill and destroy; I have come that they may have life, and have it to the full."

"I am the good shepherd. The good shepherd lays down his life for the sheep. The hired hand is not the shepherd who owns the sheep. So when he sees the wolf coming, he abandons the sheep and runs away. Then the wolf attacks the flock and scatters it. The man runs away because he is a hired hand and cares nothing for the sheep."

Self Appointed

Jesus Christ is the only gate that opens up and leads to the sheep. Any other person that does not enter through Jesus Christ is regarded as a thief or trespasser or a stranger. He does not bear heavenly authority and validation over his life to be a God's kingdom shepherd.

The sheep is Christ's and He reserves the right to appoint a shepherd over them. Any shepherd that has not been appointed by Jesus Christ or operates in the anointing of the Christ is regarded as a thief and should never be followed.

These thieves come only to steal, kill and destroy just like their father the devil. They also have the same motive at heart. They are not after the well being of the sheep. Instead, they want to mislead, rob and destroy the sheep from their ultimate purpose in God. Jesus also refers to them as bad shepherds with selfish ambitions.

Voice Identification

The sheep's ability to recognize the shepherd's voice comes with spending time with the sheep, constantly and persistently feeding them with the word of God. Voice recognition is crucial for the sheep, for direction and for leadership purposes. It also measures the intensity of doctrine, which comes over a period of time. There are many self appointed shepherds out there, so called thieves by Jesus' definition. It is therefore important for the sheep to identify with the leader's voice and know when he speaks and does not.

Jesus places great emphasis over the shepherd's voice because it is something uniquely given to mankind and cannot be copied. Its copyright is reserved and therefore it is impossible for the thief or stranger to copy or mimic overnight. The thief can also speak just as much as the shepherd can, and hence it is important for the sheep to recognize its leader's or shepherd's voice.

This principle is crucial for the survival of the sheep in the will and purposes of God. Because God speaks to us, His sheep, in a form of a sound or a peculiar voice, it is important to know when God or the devil speaks.

Laying down one's Life

Thieves will never lay down their lives or die for the sheep when the wolves come for an attack. This element is certainly missing in their genetic make-up; a sacrificial lifestyle they do not know, neither live. Instead, scripture says they tend to run away, abandon the sheep when attacks come the sheep's way, leaving the sheep vulnerable to the attack. They do not have the fatherly anointing that brings protection and provides cover. Jesus regards them as hired hands, that is, they lack the quality of ownership. They lack the quality of stewardship, crucial for a leader of God's people. This is where a broad line is drawn between them and Jesus Christ.

Earthly Minded

A true Shepherd can never do the following;
- Eat what is set aside for the flock
- Neglect
- Lead harshly
- Always demand and taking from the flock than providing.
- Never provide security and shelter.
- Dresses him/herself warmly and best meanwhile the sheep is left in the cold to suffer and die.
- What he takes from the flock is far larger and bigger than what he puts in.

- Be concerned with self-seeking pleasure at the expense of the flock.
- Always absent and leads the flock remotely
- He always sees the sheep as an inconvenience and taking much of his precious time.
- Places the flock at risk for the protection of his own.
- Be concerned with self empowering than empowering the flock.
- Most often sees him/herself as very important and matters most than the flock.

Spiritual Depth

Such shepherds are sent by the devil to confuse and ultimately destroy God's lovely people. They never show spiritual depth either in their preaching or teaching. Though they call and use the name of Jesus Christ but they are never one with Him at heart. Quite often they are worried about financial income brought in by the flock, than God's spiritual blessings descending from heaven above. Their teaching is never empowering and always revolves around the same issues. They never leave their spiritual shores to go deeper in seeking God for direction and spiritual impartation over His flock.

Prayer

They never spend time in prayer with God; neither do they encourage high intensity of prayer activities in their congregations. Preaching and self-glory is more important, though they declare prayer and fasting days activities. Their commitment is not there. Because they are so occupied with earthly activities, their prayer lifestyle is much compromised, subsequently they never know what God is saying or doing in His Body.

The Word

Though they preach, teach and even prophesy but they are never one or covenanted with the word they preach. They always preach the milk of the word, which is not sufficient for nourishing the flock. The sheep in their churches is under-nourished very thin and weak spiritually. Instead of teaching they stimulate the sheep with the word and cross over to prophesy over.

The Prophetic Word

They often give a prophetic word of exhortation around the same issues pertaining to life such as: God is saying:

- He will open great doors that will blow your mind.
- Your finances will be restored in the next few days from now.
- God has called you for greater things and never specify what things.

They always see promotions, marriages, wealth and healing coming over people lives, but none of it comes to pass. It's easier to stimulate God's sheep, especially because they are trusting and most of them are not strong and matured. Some are often desperate for breakthrough in their lives. Such false shepherds know these areas of need in the Church and therefore capitalize over these issues when they give a word of prophesy. God's anointing, power, and Scripture backup a true prophetic word from Him and always comes to pass. When a prophetic word of God comes to pass in our lives we know that it came from God, but if it does not, then it's a false word and comes from the devil.

The motive of such men is never pure at heart. They are hiding behind the grace of God, and often use His word to convince the people that they are called to do His work. One area that is most emphasized is finances. They are very sensitive around this area. They may touch other areas of the word of God but always come back to this one. Check it out for yourself.

Jude 4, 12-13, 16

For certain men whose condemnation was written about long ago have secretly slipped in among you. They are godless men, who change the grace of our God into a license for immorality and deny Jesus Christ our only Sovereign and Lord ...

These men are blemishes at your love feasts, eating with you without the slightest qualm—shepherds who feed only themselves. They are clouds without rain, blown along by the wind; autumn trees, without fruit and uprooted—twice dead. They are wild waves of the sea, foaming up their shame, wandering stars, for whom blackest darkness has been reserved forever.

*These men are grumblers and faultfinders;
they follow their own evil desires; they boast
about themselves and flatter others for their
own advantage.*

*These are the men who divide you, who
follow mere natural instincts and do not have
the Spirit.*

The Strategy to overcome

In the above verses Jude does not only highlight the characteristics of such men, but also reveals the overcoming strategy for the Church to embrace.

Jude 20-23

*But you, dear friends, build yourselves up in
your most holy faith and pray in the Holy
Spirit. Keep yourselves in God's love as you
wait for the mercy of our Lord Jesus Christ to
bring you eternal life. Be merciful to those who
doubt; snatch others from the fire and save them; to
others show mercy, mixed with fear—hating even
the clothing stained by corrupted flesh.*

May God impart a sense of discernment to help empower His Church, especially in the 21st Century. Deception is rife; the devil, with his agents, has gone all out to deceive both the mature and the immature Christians. The one who betrayed Jesus Christ was among the twelve disciples, therefore even in our days, the devil will use those around us, and often the ones closer to the vision. They show zeal yet without knowledge.

The devil is going to use people we trust to destroy us; they occupy or seek positions of influence in the leadership structure of the Church to unleash their evil motives. Such leaders are false and can never be shepherds of God's people.

Chapter 2

The Condition of the Church

Ezekiel 34:1-6

The word of the Lord came to me: "Son of man, prophesy against the shepherds of Israel; prophesy and say to them: This is what the Sovereign Lord says: Woe to the shepherds of Israel who only take care of themselves! Should not shepherds take care of the flock? You eat the curds, clothe yourselves with the wool and slaughter the choice animals, but you do not take care of the flock. You have not strengthened the weak or healed the sick or bound up the injured. You have not brought back the strays or searched for the lost. You have ruled them harshly and brutally. So they were scattered because there was no shepherd, and when they were scattered they became food for all the wild animals. My sheep wandered over all the mountains and on every high hill. They were scattered over the whole earth, and no one searched or looked for them."

In the above scripture, God expresses His deepest concern through the prophet Ezekiel regarding the condition of His sheep. God was not impressed by what the shepherds did as some continue to do so even in the 21st century. God exposes the self centred motives and ambition of the shepherds. They diverted away from the intended calling and purpose of God, and started taking care of themselves, neglecting the sheep. The condition of the sheep no longer attracted the presence of God. The condition of the sheep reflected the quality and the nature of the shepherd.

Some shepherds are so engrossed in material blessings; they have led the sheep to total spiritual negligence

It is no different in the 21st century; some of the shepherds find themselves practicing the same negligence over the sheep. They are more worried about themselves, their financial income, offshore investments, social status and fame, international travelling, general public acceptance, executive vehicles, the state of their house, the size and location of the home and the designer brand label of the clothes they wear.

These things are well and good, God is not against them, neither am I. It is indeed the same God that blesses us with these material things. However, He does not want to see His servants, the shepherds, bowing down to them and becoming bound by the same blessings. God's blessings are not intended to become a stronghold of our lives. Instead, they are meant to be enjoyed and shared amongst God's people. Shepherds need to execute proper stewarding control over these blessings instead of the other way round. Some shepherds have become so engrossed in these material blessings such that, without knowing, they have long suffered the sheep of God to total spiritual negligence.

Jesus reflected the same concern about the condition of the sheep, during the restoration of Peter:

John 21:15-18
When they had finished eating, Jesus said to Simon Peter, "Simon son of John do you truly love me more than these?" "Yes, Lord," he said, "you know that I love you."

Jesus said, "Feed my lambs." Again Jesus said, "Simon son of John, do you truly love me?" He answered, "Yes, Lord you know that I love you."

Jesus said, "Take care of my sheep." The third time he said to him, "Simon son of John, do you love me?" Peter was hurt because Jesus asked him the third time, "Do you love me?"

He said, "Lord, you know all things; you know that I love you." Jesus said, "Feed my sheep. I tell you the truth, when you were younger you dressed yourself and went where you wanted; but when you are old you will stretch out your hands, and someone else will dress you and lead you where you do not want to go."

Jesus asked Simon Peter these questions to establish the extent to which Peter will go for Jesus in looking after

His sheep. Jesus pointed out clearly in this passage of scripture that His sheep must be looked after by being fed and given care. The manner in which we look after and feed the sheep is reflective of the extent we love God. Shepherds can never lift up their holy hands to God and say they love God, when they are neglecting His greatest asset, the sheep for whom Jesus Christ died. That will be very hypocritical and totally unacceptable to God.

When a Shepherd does not lead the way God has ordained him/her, He simply removes His anointing and blessing, His glory and cover from that particular leader. When Saul failed to lead according to God's purpose and instruction, God simply shifted His glory from Saul and passed it on to David. The same can happen to a shepherd that fails to obey God when leading His sheep.

Here are the shortfalls of the shepherds that cause the sheep to wander away from God's calling and purpose.

1. **They eat the curds**. As the milk is broken into coagulants because of acid formation it forms curds, a solid edible part of the process. This means the shepherds are taking advantage over the brokenness of the sheep, forcefully taking and calling for money offering. This is offered out of guilt by the sheep. The shepherds disregard the poor or the broken state of the sheep.

2. **They clothe themselves with the wool**. Priority is on wearing expensive clothes and designer labels. The shepherds are more concerned about outward appearances, status and acceptance by the public, all at the expense of the sheep. Genuine shepherds will be more concerned about the outward look and

15

appearance of the sheep, because this is a direct reflection upon themselves.

3. **Slaughter the choice animals**. Whilst this may refer to eating the best portion of meat, it can also mean that the shepherds kill or destroy the best sheep there is within the flock.

4. **Do no take care of the sheep**. The shepherds never spend enough time nourishing, cherishing, feeding, protecting, clothing, looking after, empowering and understanding the sheep.

5. **Do not strengthen the weak sheep**. They do not teach the word, workshop the sheep and evaluate the impact of the word for the development of the sheep.

6. **Have not healed the sick**. Healing should take place at the level of spiritual, emotional, and the physically aspects of life. Scripture here refers to the healing process, not necessarily the laying on of hands and hope a miracle happens. God simply refers to a process that requires time well spent between the sheep and the shepherd.

7. **Bound up the wounded or injured ones**. This calls for the gift of kindness, selflessness, patience, gentleness, which is all-time consuming. Our modern day shepherds do not have time available at hand; media and the celebrity world is calling out loud for their attention.

8. **Have not brought back the strays or lost ones**. Evangelism has failed.

9. **Have not searched for the lost sheep**. This calls for the gift of kindness, selflessness, patience, gentleness,

which is all time consuming and our modern day shepherds do not have available at hand; media and the celebrity world is calling out loud for their attention.

10. **They have ruled them harshly and brutally**. This refers to a dictatorship leadership style that forbids input from the sheep.

The above factors clearly indicate the absence of good shepherding, unveiling the presence of self-centeredness of the shepherds who failed to look after God's flock. Subsequently, the sheep have wondered everywhere on the mountains, on every high hill and eventually scattered all over the earth.

Surely the prophet was also looking into our time. Such self proclaimed shepherds, we see on a regular basis in our congregations. Some have deceptively gathered innocent sheep around themselves, knowing very well that the whole scheme is deception.

The time has come that every shepherd should lift-up the plumb line and start measuring his/her standing position with regard to the above factorized points. These findings hold true and valid even in our present day. It is evident that we have a resurrection of the same calibre type of shepherds in our season. Clearly these men purposefully make it difficult and delay the Church from emerging victoriously against satan and his wicked schemes.

Let every shepherd so examine him/herself against these parameters: do we still have Godly driven passion, zeal, desire and willingness to serve God and lead His sheep? Or are we after the sheep's tithe and offering and motivated by such to do the will of God? If the latter holds true, then genuine repentance is the only solution for us to be restored back to God's purpose.

The plundering of the sheep is a result of the absence of good shepherds. Consequently, the sheep is exposed to wild animals which devour them. *Wild animal devouring* refers to evil spirits or devil's agents. The role of the Shepherd is to provide cover over the sheep. When the shepherd is absent then there's no cover or protection over the sheep.

God avails the following resources over His shepherds to assist them in effective leadership, these include but not limited to the following, viz.

1. Anointing to provide cover.
2. Break every stronghold.
3. Enhance breakthrough.
4. Identify resources or greener pastures.
5. Bring the sheep to a place of destiny, etc.

Therefore when a shepherd shifts from such a position of responsibility, he directly places the sheep entrusted to him/her at risk, this further opens a door of attack by the enemy.

Judgment against the Shepherds
Ezekiel 34:10-14

"This is what the sovereign Lord says: I am against the shepherds and will hold them accountable for my flock. I will remove them from tending the flock so that the shepherds can no longer feed themselves. I will rescue my

flock from their mouths, and it will no longer be food for them.

For this is what the Sovereign Lord says: "I myself will search for my sheep and look after them. As a shepherd looks after his scattered flock when he is with them, so I will look after my sheep. I will rescue them from all the places where they were scattered on a day of clouds and darkness. I will bring them out from the nations and gather them from the countries, and I will bring them into their own land. I will pasture them on the mountains of Israel, in the ravines and all the settlements in the land. I will tend them in a good pasture, and the mountain heights of Israel will be their grazing land. There they will lie down in good grazing land, and there they will feed in a rich pasture on the mountains of Israel."

Some of God's people are drying up spiritually, i.e. dying slowly spiritually as a result of the shepherd shifting from his/her spiritual occupation. Shepherds need to re-assume their spiritual position and continue with the care of the sheep. God is holding them accountable for such an act of neglect. Otherwise, God will remove them from tending the flock, so that they can no longer feed themselves off His people.

"I will rescue my flock from their mouths and will no longer be food for them."

It is very clear that there are some false shepherds whose sole mandate is to advance their own self-driven motives and interest while pretending to be good shepherds. God's judgment over such shepherds is clearly to remove them from the position of leadership so that they may no longer feed themselves off the sheep.

Here we see God replacing the vacant position of the fired shepherds with His very own presence. God will simply take over and He will not depend anymore on the shepherds. He has purposed to do it Himself instead of entrusting such a serious task to a people who are only after feeding their greedy stomachs. It is a very disappointing thing to see God casting a vote of no confidence over shepherds and totally disqualifying them from responsibility.

Judgment against the Sheep

In verse 17 we see God dealing particularly with the sheep. The sheep is not entirely free from God's judgment. God is also concerned about the sheep that is trampling over other sheep. This can refer to a sheep that is causing others to stray, intimidating, causing other sheep to default or sin, greedy and competing with other sheep. Such infighting over God's blessings results in the sheep being judged as well.

Restoration

In verse 23 God identifies the Davidic kind of shepherding as a solution. This is what God wants for His sheep. As He says, He will restore the tabernacle of David. God is raising the Davidic spirit of leadership to shepherd over the sheep in the end-times. This refers to a people who are young, never been perceived or deemed fit to serve in such positions. When we take a careful look at the life-style of David we see the following prominent features, viz.

1   He's young.
2. Unassuming.
3.   Spends most of his time with the sheep.
4. Out in the wilderness most of the time with the sheep.
5. Very brave and protective over the sheep
6. Full of Godly worship.
7. Selfless.
8. Totally committed to his responsibilities.

The sad thing is that the old order of leadership will become jealous over this new order of leadership God is raising up to take over this role. King Saul persecuted David and never allowed him to assume his position in the palace. Nothing new, the older order will always fight the new. Just like we cannot put new wine in old wine skins, otherwise there will be an explosion of the old wine-skin.

The Davidic leadership will want to see God's mandate fulfilled and will seek God's will than pursue its own. It will have the favour of God over it at all times. God will be pleased with it.

The Promise

When such leadership is in place and effectively leading, we shall see the full manifestation of the blessings of God. The trees will yield their fruits; the ground will yield its crops. From the book of ***Romans 8:19-22:***

The creation waits in eager expectation for the sons of God to be revealed. For creation was subjected to frustration, not by its own choice, but by the will of the one who subjected it, in hope that the creation itself will be liberated from its bondage to decay and brought into the glorious freedom of the children of God.

We know that the whole creation has been groaning as in pains of childbirth right up to the present time. Not only so, but we ourselves, who have the fruits of the spirit groan inwardly as we wait eagerly for our adoption as sons, the redemption of our bodies *(Romans 8:23).*

Not only are we expecting the true sons of God to manifest, but even nature eagerly awaits their full manifestation. Then shall we see the full release of God's blessings upon mankind and nature. There's an awesome breakthrough awaiting the true sons of God to take their rightful place and lead as sons. These sons are going to possess the qualities of King David's leadership.

When the true sons of God assume their place of authority and leadership and begin to reflect God in their shepherding of the sheep, then nature will see its breakthrough, and begin to yield its fruits and crops.

It is about time we began to re-embrace the sheep including the ones we have already written-off from our hearts. Let us begin all over again and reach out to the weak, feeble, injured and neglected sheep and bring them back home into the house of the Lord. Let the anointing of Elijah descend upon every Minister shepherding the flock and cause a restoration of the hearts of the fathers to the sons.

Chapter 3

The True Church

1 Kings 8:12-13, 27
"The Lord has said that He would dwell in a dark cloud; I have indeed built a magnificent temple for you, a place for you to dwell forever."

"But will God really dwell on earth? The heavens, even the highest heaven cannot contain you. How much less this temple I have built!"

After King Solomon had finished building the magnificent Temple for the Lord, he suddenly realized that if the heavens and even the highest heaven cannot contain God, how much less the temple he had built. Solomon tapped into an awesome realization that preceded his reign and season.

Even our fancy buildings are not perfect structures that can contain the presence of God. Far too long the emphasis of the Church has been the creative design of fancy building structures, auditoriums that contain large number of believers. However, this is not the case with God. He does not define a true Church in that context. Even Solomon realized that there must be a perfect suitable place for God in which to dwell forever; and that it was definitely not his fancy structured temple. The perfect place is us mankind, whom God created in His own image. We are God's dwelling place forever.

> **Ephesians 3:17**
> *... so that Christ may dwell in your hearts through faith.*

The Apostle Paul's prayer is that Jesus Christ might dwell in the hearts of the believers through faith.

Worship

The main objective of building God a temple was not so much about the fanciness of the temple structure where a large number of people could gather together. But, it was to create a formal place where people could worship God, following the Levitical order of the priesthood. The purpose of worshiping God was to invite His divine presence to come into the place of worship. Scripture says that Gods dwells in the praises of His people.

A church that truly worships is one that experiences His visitation on a regular basis

Wherever two or three people gather in His name, He is there in their midst. Therefore worship is a heavenly strategy to invite God's presence. A church that truly worships is one that experiences His visitation on a regular basis.

Col 1:18-19
And He is the head of the body, the Church; He is the beginning and the first born from among the dead, so that in everything He might have the supremacy. For God was pleased to have all His fullness dwell in Him **[Jesus Christ].**

The question is, what really pleased God about the character of Jesus Christ such that He decided to have all of His fullness or Godhead dwell in Him? When we look at the life of Jesus Christ on earth we pick up the following traits, viz.:

- A humble man
- Compassionate
- Loving and caring for people
- Reachable
- Forgiving
- Seeking God's will
- Restorer of life
- Healer
- Obedient to God
- Prayerful
- Non-discriminating
- Lives a fasted life
- Full of the word
- Lived a sinless life
- Pleasing and glorifying God always

To summarise the rest of the traits, Jesus Christ lived to please God throughout His whole life. He put God and His will first in His life. He said or did nothing, except for what He heard His Father say and do. He thus becomes a model for all mankind. We are therefore exhorted to imitate Jesus Christ.

Let us examine the current condition of the Church. Does it exhibit these traits as seen in Jesus Christ? The answer is no! The Church is negatively impacted by the following draw-backs, viz.:

- Pride
- Competition
- Sinfulness
- Disobedience
- Division
- Lack of Spiritual gifts
- Lack of faith
- No hunger for God.

Under such circumstances God cannot reveal His glory to us.

Ezek 43:4, 10, 11
⁴The glory of the Lord entered the temple through the gate facing east. ⁵Then the Spirit lifted me up and brought me into the inner court, and the glory of the Lord filled the temple. ⁶While the man was standing besides me, I heard someone speaking to me from inside the temple. ⁷He said, "Son of man, ... This is where I will live among the Israelites forever. The house of Israel will never again defile my holy name—neither they nor their kings—by their prostitution and the lifeless

*idols of their kings at their high places. ...
⁸When they placed their threshold and their
doorposts beside my doorposts, with only a
wall between me and them, they defiled my
holy name by their detestable practices. ⁹Now
let them put away from me their prostitution
and the lifeless idols of their kings, and I will
live among them forever. ¹⁰Son of man describe
the temple to the people of Israel, that they
may be ashamed of their sins. Let them
consider the plan, ¹¹and if they are ashamed of
all they have done, make known to them the
design of the temple—its arrangement, its exits
and entrances—its whole design and all its
regulations and laws. Write these down before
them so that they may be faithful to its design
and follow all its regulations."*

The glory came into the place of worship, the gateway
to His presence. As the verses indicate:

Verse 5	The Holy Spirit leads us into the inner court where the Glory dwells.
Verse 6	God's voice becomes audible to those whose hearts are open and are locked into or tuned into His presence, and suddenly hear God speak.
Verse 7	God tells us the position and the role of the Church.
Verse 8	Religion, the man-made structures, is what causes God to reject or withdraw His

	presence and ultimately becoming angry with us, the Church.
Verse 9	We need to repent or be cleansed by the blood of the Lamb, then God will dwell in our hearts forever.
Verse 10	God through His prophet Ezekiel reveals the pattern of a God house to the house of Israel. Suddenly we can all see the difference.
Verse 11	If they be ashamed; the possibility is that they may choose not to be ashamed. But if we become ashamed, then God will show us the real pattern, form and structure of true worship in His House.

Prayer

2 Chronicles 30:27

The priests and the Levites stood to bless the people, and God heard them, for their prayer reached heaven, His holy dwelling place.

Isaiah 56:7 (b)

... for my house will be called a house of prayer for all nations.

Luke 6:12.

One of those days Jesus went out to a mountainside to pray, and spent the night praying to God.

Ephesians 6:18

And pray in the spirit on all occasions with all kinds of prayers and requests. With this in mind, be alert and always keep on praying for all the saints.

A true Church is a praying Church. Prayer is one of the mechanisms designed by God to keep communication alive between mankind and Himself. As can be seen in the Scriptures above, men communicated with God in heaven where He dwells, via prayer. Prayer is an important tool in maintaining our relationship with God, updating God about our current affairs though He already knows about them.

Only sincere prayers get answered by God. Most major breakthroughs in scripture are as a result of prayer. Even Jesus Christ, while on earth, lived a prayerful life, and experienced great victories in His ministry. Therefore, the Church is exhorted to pray on all occasions with all kinds of prayers and requests.

God answers effective prayers that are rendered in line with His word. The Church is also exhorted to pray in the spirit on all occasions. Praying in the spirit is altogether a higher dimension of communicating crucial matters to God. Praying in the spirit assists in concealing important matters from satan and his agents, it bypasses that avenue, without the devil's knowledge and conveys them direct to God in Heaven. Certain prayers are not yielding results because they are aborted by the devil and his agents, even before reaching heaven.

The Church needs to grow and mature in this area of ministry. Prayer is a spiritual thing; hence we need the help of the Holy Spirit when we pray to God, because He knows how and for what to pray. He is our intercessor who prays with groans that cannot be understood. A praying Church is a victorious Church.

Prayer also goes hand in hand with fasting.

Five-Fold Gifts

Ephesians 4:11
It was He who gave some to be apostles, some to be prophets, some to be evangelists, some to be pastors and teachers, to prepare God's people for works of service, so that the body of Christ may be built up until we all reach unity in the faith and in the knowledge of the Son of God and become mature, attaining to the whole measure of the fullness of Christ.

We need the five fold ministers to impart the word of God into our lives in order for the corporate Church and individuals to grow and mature in the will of God. No impartation equals no growth. Effective growth and maturity in ministry are as a result of intense exposure to these ministries; the main diet that sustain our development.

When Jesus ascended to heaven, He gave gifts to men to help empower the Church in addition to the Holy Spirit. The gifts ought to be functionally harmonious, complementing and flowing into each other at all times. They are not given as separate entities, though in themselves, they are different in emphasis; ultimately connecting to reveal the purpose of God and Jesus Christ. The five fold ministry gifts were ordained to be fully fledged and functional within a given corporate environment, the Church structure.

They were not meant to be isolated as is the case at the moment. These gifts are interdependent of each other. The prophet or apostle or evangelist is not supposed to isolate him/herself from the rest of the other gifts.

It is inaccurate and detrimental to the sheep, if a minister who is fully-fledged in all five fold gifts is trying to operate alone. Though an apostle can be prophetic just like all the other ministers, he cannot be full time simultaneously in the second office in the five fold ministries. It is crucial for the growth and perfecting of the saints, that the Church be equally exposed to all these ministries within a given corporate structure.

It is inaccurate and detrimental to the sheep, if a minister, fully-fledged in all five fold gifts, operates alone

Jesus Christ imparted these gifts so that there can be divine order in the leadership of the Church. Ministers within the five fold should not be intimidating, competing and arrogant about their Godly given offices of operation. Instead they need to start flowing into each other for the edification and building up the body of Jesus Christ, the Church.

These gifts were also intended to advance the process of unifying the body of Jesus Christ. Leaders operating in the five-fold need to first unite, and then bring together their flock into one corporate environment of oneness. At the moment every minister is flowing alone in a different direction and so is the following flock. This division is affecting the sheep negatively. If a minister does not recognize other ministers, so does the sheep; subsequently, the body of Christ is disunited.

Leading ministers need God to help them repent of this ordeal and come back to each other and be each other's brother's keeper. No unity no blessing, but where God sees unity He commands a blessing to flow immeasurably. Unity is an expression of the Godhead, which is the Father, the Son and the Holy Spirit; therefore, it is a visible expression of the invisible heavenly unity. Unity symbolizes God and His Godhead.

Spiritual Gifts

1 Corinthians 12:7

Now to each one the manifestation of the Spirit is given for the common good. To one there is given through the Spirit the message of wisdom, to another the message of knowledge by means of the same Spirit, to another faith by the same Spirit, to another gifts of healing by that one Spirit, to another miraculous powers, to another prophecy, to another distinguishing between spirits, to another speaking in different kinds of tongues, and to still another the interpretation of tongues. All these are the work of one and the same Spirit, and he gives them to each one, just as he determines.

The Church needs to develop a genuine hunger and start placing a strong heavenly demand for the manifestation of these spiritual gifts in the Church. The heavenly supply is proportional to the earthly demand, and often supersedes it.

Spiritual gifts are vital for the flow of heavenly blessings and the health of the Church. They often symbolize the health and the well being of the Church. Every need is met within a given corporate environment of worship when these gifts are operational. They are an expression of the Holy Spirit living and moving in the Church, they are also the power weapons with which to fight the systems of darkness. They express the invisible power of God in the Church.

Discipling

Mathew 28:19

Therefore go and make disciples of all nations, baptizing them in the name of the Father and of the Son and of the Holy Spirit, and teaching them to obey everything I have commanded you.

The scripture above gives divine permission to the Church to go out and fulfil God's purpose in the earth. When we are equipped we can also go out and equip others. When we fully understand the word and can skilfully dissect and disseminate it, then we are ready to go out and make disciples out of every nation.

The word disciple has its original root from the word 'discipline.' A disciplined person is one that has been well indoctrinated in a certain system. That doctrine makes us its disciple ultimately. We need to have a belief system that can help us to be disciples.

Jesus Christ made disciples out of the twelve people by teaching them the doctrine of the kingdom of God. He made various illustrations and spoke in codes or parables. He did this in order to develop their mindsets and affirm the installation of the heavenly kingdom programme, i.e. the word of God in their minds. A true Church is a people equipped enough to go out and make disciples out of every nation, baptizing them in the name of the Father, the Son and of the Holy Spirit.

The word *making* also means to doctrinate with a valid doctrine or theology or a belief system. Baptizing in Greek is *baptizo* meaning to fully immerse in water, or soak in. Therefore let's press in to the nations for God has granted us divine permission to soak, immerse the nations into His word.

Chapter 4

The Impact and Relevance of the Church

Ezekiel 47:1-12

The man brought me back to the entrance of the temple, and I saw water coming out from under the threshold of the temple toward the east (for the temple faced the east). The water was coming down from under the south side of the temple, south of the altar. He then brought me out through the north gate and led me around the outside to the outer gate facing east, and the water was flowing from the south side.

As the man went eastward with a measuring line in his hand, he measured off thousand cubits and then led me through water that was ankle-deep. He measured off another thousand cubits and led me through water that was knee-deep. He measured off another thousand and led me through water that was up to the waist. He measured off another thousand, but now it was a river that I could not cross, because the water had risen and was deep enough to swim in—a river that no one could cross. He asked me,

"Son of man, do you see this?"

Then he led me back to the bank of the river. When I arrived there, I saw a great number of trees on each side of the river. He said to me,

"This water flows toward the eastern region and goes down into the Arabah, where it enters the Sea. When it empties into the Sea, the water there becomes fresh. Swarms of living creatures will live wherever the river flows. There will be large number of fish, because this water flows there and makes the salt water fresh; so where the river flows everything will live. Fishermen will stand along the shore, from En Gedi to En Eglaim there will be places for spreading nets. The fish will be of many kinds—like the fish of the Great Sea. But the swamps and marshes will not become fresh; they will be left for salt. Fruit trees of all kinds will grow on both banks of the river. Their leaves will not wither, nor will their fruit fail. Every month they will bear, because the water from the sanctuary flows to them. Their fruit will serve for food and their leaves for healing.

The Impact of the Water

Water represents the word of God which is continuously flowing unhindered to impact people's lives.

Water is coming out from under the threshold of the Temple flowing towards the east and southward direction. It means that God announces His righteous intentions from the platform and position of the Church. The Church is His ultimate and intimate resource through which all heavenly purposes, intended to guide and direct all mankind on the planet earth, is released.

The angel started measuring the level of the water impact to an individual. Notable is the increasing level of impact and experience after every one thousand cubits measures; from ankle deep, to knee-deep, to the waist and finally an overflowing impact that the individual cannot withstand. God is showing us that there are levels of divine experiences and encounters as we approach Him in His holy presence. God wants to pour Himself out into the Church and ultimately into the whole world. The first people chosen to experience His divine visitation is the Church.

God is showing us that the world's actual source of life and meaning is found in the Church

The whole purpose of the word of God is to bring the Church to the place where God's presence is overwhelmingly and tangibly felt, like a river that we cannot cross. Our encounter with God should be such that we cannot afford to stand in His presence but flow. As a Church we need to go through these divine experiences, observed at different levels. Such encounters are crucial for our growth in the Lord.

The Impact of the River

The river in this regard represents the Church of God and the sea represents the world. The power of the flow of the Church should be such that nothing can stop its impact in the world. In the scripture we see trees growing along the river bank. The life that comes from within the Church should affect the surroundings and bring life to dead situations.

Again, we see the river flowing towards the sea and causing the sea water to become fresh. The Church should be moving away from its comfort zone into the world where relevant impact is expected and needed. The relevance of the Church is to bring flavour, refreshing and life to the world. In other words, the Church is the world's true source of life, refreshment and meaning. Our core purpose should be to reach out to the dying world and make disciples out every nation and baptize them in the name of the Father, the Son and of the Holy Spirit. The trees growing along the bank of the river represent the people that will be born again as a result of the preaching of the word of God. The newly saved believers are the spiritual offspring of the Church, the Body of Christ.

The Church is the world's true source of life, refreshment and meaning

We are living in times where people suffer from the struggles of stress, depression, anxiety, poverty, wars, limited resources, dire spiritual famine and competition for limited resources. In such situations the Church needs to become significant and effectively address such issues. Our prayers must, over and above, be accompanied by actions. The provision for life related issues such as health, peace, stability, hope, future, etc. should come through the channels of the Church. The Church ensures that the will of God is done on earth as it is in heaven. The heavenly order affects and changes the earthly order. Right now the whole world is negatively affected by the HIV and AIDS and other pandemics that are claiming millions of lives. The Church should, therefore, be the genuine voice and the solution that comes from God.

Commitment

Acts 2:42-47

They devoted themselves to the apostles' teaching and to the fellowship, to the breaking of bread and to prayer. Everyone was filled with awe, and many wonders and miraculous signs were done by the apostles. All the believers were together and had everything in common. Selling their possessions and goods, they gave to anyone as he had need. Everyday they continued to meet together in the temple courts. They broke bread in their homes and ate together with glad and sincere hearts, praising God and enjoying the favour of all the people. And the Lord added to their number daily those who were being saved.

The standard of teaching the word of God ought to raise up the Church to new dimensions of impact. The Church must commit as well as avail herself to the intense and in-depth levels of teaching and learning the word of

God so that she comes to a place of full maturity and be skilful at the execution of the word. The Holy Spirit is pouring out fresh revelation with emphasis on the word of God. The Church ought to be experiencing a divine level of this out-pouring of the rain of the word of God.

The early Church became increasingly more effective and meaningful in the society when they devoted themselves to the *teachings, fellowship, breaking of the bread and prayer.*

- The apostles' teachings helped them to be more knowledgeable and mature as Disciples of Christ.
- The fellowship on daily basis helped in strengthening and encouraging the process of learning.
- The breaking of bread helped in the nourishing and equal distribution of available resources.
- Prayer helped them remain focused, anointed, sensitized to the Holy Spirit and attaining to much needed breakthrough from God.

Retaining this pattern excited God to a point where He added to their number daily those who were being saved. While the Church did its part, God did His as well by adding to the Church and bringing increase. Therefore, we should not worry ourselves with strategies to boost our membership; that's for God to do. Ours is to stay in the will of God and do it. Church growth is therefore directly dependent on the prayer, commitment, fellowship, spiritual sensitivity, obedience, oneness and equal sharing.

The selling of possessions by some of the members of the Church to help those that were in need clearly reflected a character of giving, caring and loving. The Church should be people conscious and oriented toward people relationships than material driven and chasing after prosperity agendas. The current Church has seriously lost these attributes as reflected by the early Church. She has since seen no growth in terms of membership, and marginal maturity in terms of spiritual values. Prosperity and self-enriching seems to be the fundamental emphasis of the current Church.

Prayerfulness

2 Chronicles 30:27

The priests and the Levites stood to bless the people, and God heard them, for their prayer reached heaven, his holy dwelling place.

One of the spiritual obligations to keep the church alive, fruitful and effective is praying. A non-praying Church is non-existent and non-effective Church. Without prayer it is difficult to understand the purposes and intentions of God.

Prayer keeps the communication lines between God and His people open. It opens up the spiritual channel and connects us directly to our heavenly Father. It is when we pray effectively and fervently according to God's word and God's will that we receive the answers and solutions to our problems and challenges respectively. Even Jesus Christ prayed while on earth in order to be able to overcome the devil's schemes and attacks. Through prayer and fasting Jesus was able to bring deliverance and major breakthroughs over people's lives. Towns and cities opened up to receive Him and His ministry.

> *Colosians 4:2-3*
> *Devote yourselves to prayer, being watchful and thankful. And pray for us, too, that God may open a door for our message, so that we may proclaim the mystery of Christ, for which I am in chains.*

Through prayer we are able to break and pull down territorial strongholds thereby opening the gates of towns and cities to the impact of God. Prayer is the key to open up closed doors and country gates that would otherwise never open up to let God in. Some of us are called to distant lands and nations, therefore we need more fervent prayers to help unlock these areas, and go in to preach and teach the gospel of Jesus Christ.

The prayer of the righteous ones avails much. When God's children pray, God grants their prayers accordingly. Prayer is a heavenly tool designed for God's church to use in order to attain great results. We can pray as individuals or in a corporate gathering for all our needs and those of others. Through prayer we are able to address any and all issues pertaining to life itself.

> *Romans 8:26*
> *In the same way, the Spirit helps us in our weakness. We do not know what we ought to*

pray for, but the Spirit himself intercedes for us with groans that words cannot express.

God allows us to pray in our earthly languages. However, He prefers it when we pray in the spirit being led and directed by His Holy Spirit, who is able to intercede with groans and words we cannot even utter. Our earthly languages have in themselves limitations; there are deep spiritual issues and dynamics that we cannot pray for in our languages. Simply, there is not enough vocabulary to express them to God. However, when pray in the Spirit and through the Holy Spirit there are no limitations. He understands the heavenly language and can accurately express to God the Father that for which we are praying at any given instance.

Psalm 17:6
I call on you, O God, for you will answer me, give ear to me and hear my prayer.

When sometimes our prayers do not yield expected results, we marvel and remain with lots of questions toward God. But, that's not how it should be; God answers every prayer. We need to grow and understand that some of the answers we expect from God are in a form of communication, whereby God answers by literally telling us what, and how to do it.

God does not do things for us all the time. There are times when he expects us to listen to His instruction and do things on our own. This is where we often fail, because some Christians are not good spiritual listeners. Our ears are still deaf with regards to spiritual information. We are in need, therefore, of unclogging to help us understand and appropriate spiritually discerned information.

When we pray God listens, likewise, when God speaks back to us we need to listen. It is a two way process. Prayer is not commanding God what to do, when to do it, and how to do it. Often times that is the attitude we have embraced regarding praying to such an extant that, some of us, are used to banging heavenly doors, rocking heavenly gates to catch God's attention. This is not how we ought to pray to our loving God. There is no need for all this aggression when praying. Prayer is an intimate mode of communication with God. It is a powerful yet delicate and sensitive form of communication.

There are deep spiritual issues and dynamics that we cannot pray for in our earthly languages

God will amaze us someday when He reveals to us how every prayer gets answered, but our own immaturity has hindered us from seeing such results.

The word *watchful* above (*Col. 4:2*) refers to the spiritual opening of the eyesight. This goes beyond seeing in the natural, which is limited. It transcends into dimensions beyond human comprehension. Its emphasis lies in the comprehension of what is spiritually discerned, that which no eye can see except the spirit. Jesus Christ was saying that we must carefully study our environment and observe the changes, then pray in line with that.

Proverbs 15:29

The Lord is far from the wicked but he hears the prayer of the righteous.

It is important to note that God pays more attention when His righteous children pray, than when sinners do. This is because sinners do not have a living relationship with Him and neither are they God's children, nor Abraham's seed. Most importantly is that, sinners do not have the Holy Spirit as seal over their lives. On the other hand the righteous have the Holy Spirit seal and are by promise the children of Abraham and sons of God. Therefore, God pays more attention to those who are called by His name. Typical of any father, He will first protect and pay more attention to his children and everybody else later.

1 Peter 3:12
For the eyes of the Lord are on the righteous and his ears are attentive to their prayer.

This scripture backs everything discussed above. As a father, God is totally responsible for our lives, He never slumbers nor sleeps; His eyes are constantly watching over His property.

Acts 12: 5, 11
So Peter was kept in prison, but the Church was earnestly praying to God for him. Then Peter came to himself and said, "Now I know without doubt that the Lord sent his angel and

rescued me from Herod's clutches and from everything the Jewish people were anticipating."

The earnest prayer of the righteous prevailed much, when the Church corporately prayed in agreement for Peter. God answered miraculously by sending His angel to rescue Peter. Their prayers triggered a heavenly intervention. God was moved and tasked the angel to go and rescue Peter from prison. There are no limits in terms of what God can do for us. Nothing is too hard or impossible or difficult with our God. God is not limited by earthly circumstances; they were created by Him anyway. There is nothing on earth that does not obey the voice and the command of the Lord.

Ephesians 6:18-19
And pray in the spirit on all occasions with all kinds of prayers and requests. With this in mind, be alert and always keep on praying for all the saints. Pray also for me, that whenever I open my mouth, words may be given me so that I will fearlessly make known the mystery of the gospel, for which I am an ambassador in chains. Pray that I may declare it fearlessly, as I should.

Apostle Paul was charging the church in Ephesus to always pray in the spirit, because when we pray in the spirit, we are communicating crucial issues beyond the comprehension of the devil. The devil cannot hear us when we pray in the language of the spirit; he has no access code to that language. Therefore, he cannot counterfeit and cripple our prayers.

There is an element of alertness mentioned in this scripture which I believe is crucial in our season whenever we pray. Being alert is being extra careful or being spiritually sensitive so as to detect changes, effect them as we pray as expected by God. There are times as we pray that God requires us to change the subject and include praying for other needs. We need to be sensitive all the time to the Holy Spirit in order to be able to make such adjustments.

Prayer plays a crucial part in the ministry of the word. Here, Apostle Paul requests the saints to pray for him, that he may be given divine or words of wisdom and boldness whenever he would open his mouth to speak. This is very crucial. At times we do not know what we ought to say and how to say it, but as we pray the Holy Spirit then suddenly gives us utterances in line with the purposes of God.

James 5:15:
And the prayer offered in faith will make the sick person well; the Lord will raise him up.

A prayer offered in faith is able to bring divine healing to the sick and bring him/her back to life. Our prayers have been endorsed with so much of power that there is nothing God cannot do for His children when they pray according to His will. Through prayer we are able to release heavenly resources and channel them to a specific need.

Mark 9:29
He replied, "This kind can come forth by nothing, but by prayer and fasting."
(King James Version)

Here we encounter a situation whereby the disciples were sent out by Jesus Christ to go and exercise their faith.

God has opened doors for His people to come into influential government positions and bring about change

They came across a boy who was demon possessed and prayed over him, but he could not get delivered. So they came back to report. Jesus responded by saying to them that they needed to fast and pray to see result manifesting. What Jesus Christ was teaching here is very important even today. Jesus was simply saying, 'Guys you need to ascertain certain conditions then determine the required kind of a solution. Do not be religious in your approach; use your gift of discernment to determine what is required in a given situation.'

There are times where you need to engage the devil deeper than you would under normal circumstances. There are times where prayer alone is not sufficient, we need to couple it or enhance it with fasting. Fasting is the catalyst to our prayer. It boosts prayer and shortens the period to obtaining breakthroughs. Fasting activates powers and support mechanism required in the spirit in order to achieve results in the natural. We need to live a fasted lifestyle daily, because we are surrounded by demanding conditions. People come to Church with all sorts of troubles, sicknesses and complex conditions. There's no sickness or disease that God cannot heal, even the most incurable diseases, they surrender whenever we pray earnestly to God. Through prayer God is able to heal and deliver.

Relevance in Government Structures

Daniel 6:1-3

It pleased Darius to appoint 120 satraps to rule throughout the kingdom, with three administrators over them, one of whom was Daniel. The satraps were made accountable to them so that the king might not suffer loss. Now Daniel so distinguished himself among the administrators and the satraps by his exceptional qualities that the king planned to set him over the whole kingdom.

In this passage of scripture, we encounter Daniel, a servant of God, who is a distinguished administrator. He portrayed exceptional qualities that earned him the highest position among other administrators. It was God's plan to use Daniel to invade the governmental system of King Nebuchadnezzar. God's plan about using His people to bring a God favourable change in government structures has not changed. The favour of God over Daniel's life opened greater doors, not only for Daniel, but also for God to reveal and display His power over that nation.

Current political and governmental systems do not have honour, recognition and or even fear for God.

49

Policies that have to do with governance over people are drafted and accepted without or limited influential input from the Church. I believe God has opened similar doors for His people to come into influential governmental positions and to bring about change. God is looking for people who will manifest and represent His authority in such structures. Even nature is awaiting such true sons of God to take their rightful place in governing authorities.

It is time for the Church to be bold enough to stand up and declare what God is saying, just like Daniel who dared to be different, took a stance and represented his God. The Church should not be conforming to such godless policies but should become God's voice in government structures. Though God is no respecter of persons, He can use anybody whether saved or not, but He would prefer to exalt His Church and bring a solution through it.

Relevance in Socio-Economic Structures

Genesis 41: 41-43, 47

So Pharaoh said to Joseph, "I hereby put you in charge of the whole land of Egypt." Then Pharaoh took his signet ring from his finger and put it on Joseph's finger. He dressed him in robes of fine linen and put a gold chain around his neck. He had him ride in a chariot as his second-in-command, and men shouted before him, "Make way!" Thus he put him in charge of the whole land of Egypt.

During the seven years of abundance the land produced plentifully. Joseph collected all

> *the food produced in those seven years of abundance in Egypt and stored it in the cities. In each city he put the food grown in the fields surrounding it.*

God is currently downloading the same favour and the technology of Joseph over the Church today. There are individuals upon whom God is releasing similar anointing to accomplish even greater things than those accomplished by Joseph. The anointing of Joseph is pouring over the corporate body of Jesus Christ, the Church. Locked within the system of Joseph was the divine ability to decode spiritual mysteries and skilfully articulate them for human understanding. His ability to exercise his spiritual gift earned him a high ranking position, being the second in charge of the whole land of Egypt. Joseph was able to translate Pharaoh's dream and skilfully applied its interpretation to help rescue the socio-economy status of Egypt.

Quite often than not we always see the future as bringing hope and prosperity. However, this was not the situation in this particular case study. The future was going to negatively impact the socio-economic status of the country. Therefore God through Joseph was able to rescue the people of Egypt. The same principle holds for our economies today. God uses, and still wants to use more of His people, to predict rescue and bring prosperity in today's socio-economic structures.

The Store House (Principle of Tithing)
Malachi 3:10

Bring the whole tithe into the storehouse, that there may be food in my house. Test me in this, says the Lord Almighty, and see if I will not throw open the floodgates of heaven and pour out so much blessing that you will not have room enough for it.

Often we refer to this scripture when its time to collect tithes and offering in the Church. But I believe we have not done justice to it in trying to understand its depth. God is commanding that the whole tithe be brought into the storehouse, so that there may be food for everyone including His servants. He did not say bring in the whole tithe to my servant so that he may only have food and be blessed. The tithe is intended to come into the storehouse of the Lord so that there may be resources as required. The primary principle behind the tithing concept is self-empowering and sustainability. As God is promising above, *"He will throw open the floodgates of heaven and pour out so much blessing that we will not have room enough for it."* This means taking good care of His appointed servants and as well as the whole congregation at large.

Food in this passage of scripture doesn't only refer to food as provided by soup kitchens, but could also refer to packets of groceries, clothes, fresh vegetables and fruits, staple food, money and job opportunities, etc. Many of our Churches do not have these storehouses, simply because we do not understand the principle underlying the tithe. A storehouse is an extra or additional room, maybe big or small, but it must be there for every Church. When somebody in the Church is poor, or lacks finances, or in need of clothes or food, or fiancés, the Church should not panic when these needs suddenly crop up, but rather go into the storehouse and retrieve that which is needed.

I believe once we understand this principle on tithing, we will be very relevant in our society. In In certain instances you'll find that most people who are in need are the very same ones who are tithing their monies to the Church. Ironic enough, the Church cannot assist its own members whenever they are in need. Show me a storehouse of a Church, and I will tell you if they are tithing to God or not. Our own fellow beloved members should not experience lack, when they are actually paying their tithes honestly. The Church should provide and take care of such needs. That is the whole purpose of the tithing. The Church needs to first take care of its faithful members, and then flow out to its neighbouring societies.

God still wants to use more of His people to predict, rescue and bring prosperity in today's socio-economic structures

Charity begins at home, in as much as the judgment of God will first begin with the Church then to the world at large. In this century we need to clearly define these concepts, so that we can be relevant and impact our societies with great significance.

The Location of the Church

God is speaking and addressing each of the churches based on their geographical location. He also is conveying crucial messages for theses Churches through their spiritually appointed territorial Angels. The role of the

Angels is to guard and disseminate God's messages to the churches; they are also responsible for assisting the churches in their warfare.

One important thing to be noted is that God called the churches according to the names of their geographical location.

Chapter 5

Challenges Facing the Church

Understanding the Times and the Seasons
1 Chronicles 12:32
... men of Issachar, who understood the times and knew what Israel should do.

God had blessed the men of Issachar with a gift of understanding and knowledge. These men were very important in Israel. Israel knew what to do and when to do it, because the sons of Issachar played a very crucial role interpreting the seasons for and on behalf of the nation of Israel. These men, I believe, were used as a picture of the Church in modern times.

The Church should be playing a similar role in her society today. However, the challenge facing the Church today, is to understand the times, the seasons and knowing what to do. Judging by the sequence of events, certain elements of the Church are maturing faster than the others and have better knowledge about interpreting the times and knowing what to do, than others do. Certain members still display an attribute of immaturity and a deep lack of understanding God's time and seasons. Lack of understanding hinders one from attaining to knowledge.

In *Matthew 24:1-44* Jesus reveals the signs of the End of the Age to His disciples. Let me select a few verses from this passage:

Verse 32

"Now learn this lesson from the fig tree: As soon as its twigs get tender and its leaves come out, you know that summer is near. Even so, when you see all these things, you know that it is near, right at the door. I tell you the truth, this generation will certainly not pass away until all these things have happened."

Verse 42

"Therefore keep watch, because you do not know on what day your Lord will come."

Jesus' emphasis on the teaching of understanding the seasons is by carefully studying and observing certain key blue print elements that are designed as guidelines for mankind. Though we do not know the exact time of His second coming, we have been well armed with the visible signs of things that will take place before Jesus comes back. This information is good enough to prepare the Church for the second coming of the Messiah. Jesus gave us enough guidelines to help His Church prepare for His second coming.

Right now the Church is at a place where she needs to fully understand this season. Things happening around her require that she applies spiritual technology to survive. She must be relevant and make more disciples out every nation. Currently the Church is moving in circles or going around the same mountain over and over again, because she has lost sight, vision and purpose. This hinders her frm hearing the voice of her Shepherd, Jesus Christ.

A new season has dawned. The body of Christ at large needs to grasp it and make necessary adjustments to align and comply with the requirements of the new season. The essence of understanding the times is beyond emphasis.

Matthew 25:1-13
"At that time the kingdom of heaven will be like ten virgins who took their lamps and went out to meet the bridegroom. Five of them were foolish and five were wise. The foolish ones took their lamps but did not take any oil with them. The wise, however, took oil in jars along with their lamps. The bridegroom was a long time in coming, and they all became drowsy and fell asleep.

At midnight the cry rang out: 'Here's the bridegroom! Come out to meet him!' Then all the virgins woke up and trimmed their lamps. The foolish ones said to the wise, 'Give us some of your oil; our lamps are going out.'

'No,' they replied, 'there may not be enough for both us and you. Instead, go to those who sell oil and buy some for yourselves.' But while they were on their way to buy oil, the bridegroom arrived. The virgins who were

ready went in with him to the wedding banquet. And the door was shut.

"Later the others also came, 'Sir! Sir!' they said. 'Open the door for us!' But he replied, 'I tell you the truth I don't know you.'
"Therefore keep watch because you do not know the day or the hour."

The virgins are a reflection of the Church in the last days. It will split and result in the formation of two types, called the foolish and the clever. A Church classified as the clever one will be able to position and ready itself for the coming of the groom, Jesus Christ. Meanwhile, the foolish Church will be caught out unprepared and ill positioned spiritually. Jesus' emphasis is that the Church should be ready at all times, for she does not know the day or the hour of His second coming. In this particular case study, it is clear that the foolish virgins were disqualified to enter in with the bride groom, and were further disqualified from his presence, when he announced 'I do not know you.'

Jesus is teaching the end time church a powerful lesson. Despite our human or carnal efforts to get ready to meet Him, if we miss the timing of His arrival, we will be a disqualified bride. The door will be shut right on our faces. God is totally worried about our spiritual preparedness than the carnal one. The Church (bride) has to make herself ready to meet with the Lamb of Glory.

What is God Saying Now—The Church must be Newly Defined

> *Romans 13: 11-14*
> *And do this, understanding the present time. The hour has come for you to wake up from your slumber, because our salvation is nearer now than when we first believed. The night is nearly over; the day is almost here. So let us put aside the deeds of darkness and put on the armor of light. Let us behave decently, as in the daytime, not in orgies and drunkenness, not in sexual immorality and debauchery, not in dissension and jealousy. Rather, clothe yourselves with the Lord Jesus Christ, and do not think about how to gratify the desires of the sinful nature.*

The root meaning of the word *understanding* above refers to intimate knowledge or exact knowledge. It is also similar to a man knowing his wife in marriage. God therefore, demands the Church to come to a place of full understanding of the times. The Church has entered a crucial hour or a new season in the spirit. Thus God demands of His Church to catch this wake up call, otherwise we are going to misrepresent His Kingdom on earth and also miss the second coming of the Lord Jesus Christ.

The Church has to wake up from slumber, for behold our salvation is nearer now than we first believed. One thing is that when a person has fallen into a deep asleep, he eventually dreams, reflecting an earthly disconnection from God. Though he does not have control over what is happening to him during this spiritual connection, he is merely dreaming objects. So when he is dreaming everything is spontaneously happening around him, without his intellectual or psychological participation.

God is saying that we need to wake up and take full responsibility around us and fulfil His mandate in the earth. We cannot only be dreamers. We need to go beyond dreaming and bring all those dreams and visions into realization and manifestation. There is a time for dreaming and shouting about it, but there's also another time when God is expecting us to live those dreams. The demand upon us as the latter Church is that we need to bring into fulfilment what our forefathers of faith saw afar as a promise but never inherited.

The demand on the latter Church is to bring into fulfillment what our forefathers of faith saw afar

The word *salvation* refers to Jesus Christ. He is almost drawing closer to His second coming; therefore we need to be ready as His Bride. For we know that He is coming for a spotless Bride without blemishes who has been made ready for the final wedding with the Lamb of Glory.

The night is almost over; behold a new day is dawning. Therefore let us behave as those living in the day. Put aside all the deeds of darkness, including hypocrisy, malice and sexual immorality. God is calling out His Church to manifestation of Jesus Christ. We all know the light of the day exposes everything. It is that time whereby the Church of God is being revealed upon the face of the earth.

The instruction to put on Jesus Christ refers to three things. Firstly, this speaks of the glory of God covering His Church. What we put on will ultimately define us to the world in which we live, since people first see us before they hear us. God is bringing us to a place of divine renewal in Christ Jesus. This process is a very crucial one, since the Church must be covered by the Glory of Jesus Christ.

Secondly, God wants to reveal the promised end-time glory of His Son and He is going to do it via the corporate Church. The Church is entering a new era right now. This is an era whereby we are going to see the last flashes of all sorts of evil under the sun; the world is becoming more evil by the day. The devil is doing so in contravention of the dawning of the new day that marks the revealing of the true Church. As God is declaring a new day, the devil will counter by declaring an hour of darkness. The Church should be careful not to get caught up in this process; she needs to focus on her key role of putting on the garment called Jesus Christ. God will take care of satan and all his schemes.

The Church neesd to focus on her key role of putting on the garment called Jesus Christ

Thirdly, 'putting on Jesus Christ' means putting on the full armour of faith. This is the final preparation for a defined spiritual war that must take place. This is the end-time war, that must take place to defeat all systems and schemes and powers of satan. In order to engage the enemy effectively and win over him, the Church needs a structural rearrangement, and this is defined by the restoration of the Davidic Tabernacle.

The Primary Mandate of the Church

Matthew 28:18-20

Then Jesus came to them and said, "All authority in heaven and on earth has been given to me. Therefore go and make disciples of all nations, baptizing them in the name of the Father and of the Son and of the Holy Spirit, and teaching them to obey everything I have commanded you. And surely I am with you always, to the very end of the age."

This is the full mandate of the Church today. We cannot divert or side-track from this mission; it must be accomplished no matter what. Of course the devil will attempt to nullify it from coming to pass, but he will lose out big time. Jesus' intention is to see all nations of the earth made His disciples and baptized in the name of the Father, the Son and of the Holy Spirit and finally be empowered with kingdom knowledge. For the Church to accomplish this mission, she has to first realize that all power and authority in heaven and on earth resides within sender who is Jesus Christ.

The Church has to make this mandate her primary one; never resting till the mission is accomplished. This command has to take deep rooting within the heart of every believer. Time is running out, many souls out there are dying at a high accelerated rate. We need to embrace a fresh momentum and do a quantum leap in the spirit to accomplish this mission. God is awaiting the Church to come back and tell Him what is required to fully bring this task to pass. We need to ask God for the power of translation beyond human technology to speed up this process.

What also seems to be the challenge for the Church today; is the types of doctrinal teachings that we teach the sheep. Most often than not, such teachings do not glorify God but exalts and personalize an individual who ministers and forces the sheep to identify with that particular individual minister. The Church at large needs to understand that this mission defies every other human self-centred mission, there's no room for men to glorify and built themselves kingdoms other than the one Jesus Christ has established by the shedding of His precious blood. We all need to come together as one, and help each other to accomplish the task.

The Depth of the Word
John 1:1
In the beginning was the Word, and the Word was with God, and the Word was God.

The word of God is equal to God Himself made manifest in the form of the word. God began everything during the creation process with the word, and He shall also end everything using the word. The word of God is the only way through which we can discover the deepest secrets in the heart of God. Therefore, the shallow we are in the word, the shallow we become in the knowledge and the fellowship with God.

God's word is the only way to discover the deepest secrets in God's heart

The only way to discover God's purposes, aims and objectives is through His Word. Spending more time and fellowship in the word of God, will help mature and fully develop Christians in the knowledge of God. It is about time we start spending more valuable time in the partaking of the word, than doing anything else.

Psalm 119:11
I have hidden your word in my heart that I might not sin against you.

People who are deep in the word of God, have the potential and capacity to hide the word of God deep in their hearts. The shallow we are in the word, the shallow the word will be placed in our hearts. The word of God has the power to keep and guard us from sinning against Him. Jesus Christ reiterated the same to His disciples, saying "a man is not defiled by the food he eats, but by what comes out from his mouth." *(Matthew 15:11)*. It is the words we speak with our mouths that defile and condemn us and not food necessarily. Scripture says we shall be judged by every idle word we speak *(Matthew 12:36)*. Therefore, we can see that God has placed a strong emphasis on His word than on anything else.

When we are full of God's word in our hearts, the same we draw out against the enemy when he comes to tempt us. However, when we are empty of His word, nothing comes out. We need to go deeper in the word of God, to discover God's secrets and purposes for our lives. The question is how deep have we hidden the word of God in our hearts? The depth of God's word in our hearts is based on our capacity to receive it. We need to create depth for the word deposit in our hearts for God's word.

> *2 Timothy 2:15b*
> *A workman ... who correctly handles the word of truth.*

Apostle Paul's instruction to Timothy is that he may grow to become a workman who correctly handles the word of truth. It takes practice and thorough exercise in the word for an individual Christian to become a workman (Word Specialist) that is able to rightfully divide the word of God. Paul is careful about Timothy's accuracy of handling and dissecting the word of God. It says in *Hebrews 4:12,*

> *"For the word of God is living and active. ... it penetrates even to dividing soul and spirit, joints and marrow; it judges the thoughts and attitudes of the heart."*

If we are not skilful in the word, we can default in its application, and thereby cause lot of irreparable spiritual damage. This may lead to people's destinies negatively affected and the ultimate plan of God hindered in their lives. Therefore, the challenge boldly confronting Christians in the twenty first century is growing up and growing deep in the word of God. We need to do spiritual audit in the following areas, viz,

- What are the current updates; are we preaching the same stuff just different days?
- Are we getting deeper in the word?
- Can we measure our intensity of preaching and teaching?
- Are the people we lead getting immersed in the word; or, is the word still hanging above their heads?

The Role of the Church in dealing with HIV and AIDS and other Diseases

2 Chronicles 7:13-14
When I shut up the heavens so that there is no rain, or command locusts to devour the land or send a plague among my people, if my people, who are called by my name, will humble themselves and pray and seek my face and turn from their wicked ways, then will I hear from heaven and will forgive their sin and will heal their land.

Our God is a God of healing, as one can see from the scripture above, there are times when God becomes angry with His people for reason of disobedience and subsequently inflict them with plagues. However, He does this for various reasons, to teach them a lesson, get their attention to repent from committing evil acts and to hinder them from worshiping other false gods.

In the case of HIV and AIDS I believe that God foretold of it through His servants the prophets, who did proclaim it to the nations at that time. The HIV and AIDS is as a direct result of explicit unfaithfulness with regards to sexual commitment. Such an act is offensive and punishable by God. Again through this epidemic God is trying to convey a message to His people that they should remain faithful towards their Godly ordained married partners. Sex in scripture is allowed only in the premise of the marriage covenant and nowhere else, nor by any other alternative means allowed. Sex outside marriage is a sin; therefore, punishable. God created a man for one woman and demands of them to be faithful to each other at all times during the time they are married.

Due to man's disobedience and unfaithfulness, God has had to afflict mankind with this epidemic. The big question though is; is this epidemic curable? The answer is YES, through God who heals all our diseases. Nothing is impossible with God, He is able to heal and totally eradicate such a disease from our bodies. On one condition, that we humble ourselves and pray and seek His face and turn from our wicked ways. Then God will hear from heaven and will heal this epidemic called HIV and AIDS.

Job 5:18
For He wounds, but He also binds up; He injures, but His hands also heal.

From the scripture above, it is very clear that the same God is able to wound or injure, binds us up or heal us.

Eccl 3:3
A time to kill and a time heal, a time to tear
down and a time to build.

There's time and a season for everything under the sun. God created all these, no situation lasts forever. When a person is afflicted with sickness or disease, it is just a matter of time, he will get healed again. God does not take pleasure in seeing His people walking up and down seeking for healing deliverance or crying for it all the time.

Jeremiah 33:6
Nevertheless, I will bring health and healing to
it; I will heal my people and will let them
enjoy abundant peace and security.

God's intention is to bring and provide healing to His people. God wants only the best for His people. There is no such thing as God enjoys seeing His people sick and the poor going around begging. God is a good God, and wants the same and the best for His people.

Matthew 10:8
Heal the sick, raise the dead, cleanse those
who have leprosy, drive out demons. Freely
you have received, freely give.

Here again Jesus' mission was not only to preach about God's kingdom, but to heal the sick, breaking bondages, confinements and addictions by His anointing, thereby setting God's people free. God's people should not pay a price for deliverance or healing. Jesus Christ has already paid this price in full. We should not be going around telling God's people to plant seeds of faith for their healing or deliverance, God's gifts are free to us, and He expects to offer them as services freely to His beloved people.

Therefore, HIV and AIDS can be cured and is curable in the House of the Lord for free. God has provided a cure for this epidemic through His Kingdom, so that all the glory will return back to Him. He did it so as to glorify and exalt His Church in the earth, so that all mankind can see and witness His power operating through the Church.

Church and Politics

The Church of God has a crucial role to play in politics, but she must not or never become political. It is the plan of God to reveal His purposes through the Church. This is the avenue and the stance that the Church needs to maintain. It is the Church's responsibility to represent the voice and the mind of God in the earth. I believe the Church must assume her advisory role in governing structures but avoid getting caught up in the political issues. The Church is neither God nor Government in the earth; her participation in politics is limited only to what God intends to do. Otherwise she needs to continue in her task of making disciples of the nations of the earth. She has a crucial spiritual role to play.

Certain issues touching human lives can best be addressed by the Church as she represents the Creator of mankind in the earth.

God and Technology

Genesis 6:13

So God said to Noah, "I am going to put an end to all people, for the earth is filled with violence because of them. I am surely going to destroy both them and the earth. So make yourself an ark of cypress wood; make rooms in it and coat it with pitch inside and out. This is how you are to build it: The ark is to be 140 metres long, 23 metres wide and 13.5 metres high. Make a roof for it and finish the ark to within half a metre of the top. Put a door in the side of the ark and make lower, middle and upper decks.

It must be noted that this was the very first time Noah heard of the word Ark, let alone knowing how it looked like. Through the invention of the Ark, God showed mankind that technology originates from Him above. Our God is father of all technologies on earth. God didn't surprise Noah with the idea of building the Ark, but empowered him with wisdom and understanding. Noah was instructed to bring forth into reality the concept of the Ark according to the way God instructed him.

Through the Ark formation God introduced the system of accurate measurements, placements, water engineering, architecture, etc. The system of export and import trade via the shores of our nations and countries finds its origin from the Ark architectural engineering. Technology comes from the heart of God, the creator of all things. The earth and all its fullness belongs to our God.

Nothing existing by mistake on earth, for the earth and all its fullness belongs to God. God has direct control over every thing, from mankind to technology that has made man great. All wisdom comes from God - meaning all forms of technology originate from the heart of God. Everything on earth was created by God, to help mankind live a better life, worship God without difficulty. Everything around us is pointing towards God. The technology around us should help us worship and revere God at all times.

> *Romans 11:34*
> *Who has known the mind of the Lord? Or who has been His counsellor? Who has ever given to God, that God should repay him? For from Him and through Him and to Him are all things. To Him be the glory for ever! Amen.*

All things referring to everything plus technology come from God. We therefore cannot try and use technology to discover or verify the existence of God, who created all things. Technology is limited no matter how advanced it is, but it is limited in terms of discovering or validating the presence of God.

Also, mankind cannot rely on technology to attain perfection. True human kind perfection is derived from the realization and acceptance of our weaknesses and limitations, repentance from sinfulness, and thus allowing Jesus Christ to perfect us. It's a spiritual thing; our carnal nature will battle to comprehend it. God perfected all things through Jesus Christ, thus only through Christ can we be made perfect. Human cloning is also not a perfect art towards creating the very finest human being with perfect features in the right places. Man's idea of perfection is not like God's and is also very limited in its attempt.

Solomon became the wisest man on earth, by asking God for wisdom. The queen of Sheba came to audit Solomon's wisdom and also to verify the source of his wisdom. In her findings, Solomon outclassed her standards of evaluation and passed every test given to him. Again there was God Almighty in the background, helping Solomon to excel in these tests.

Chapter 6

Fullness of the Times

What does the fullness of the times mean to the Church? How is the Church supposed to conduct herself when times would have reached their fullness? What is expected of the Church when times will have reached their fullness? The scriptures below and their explanations will, by the Spirit of God, help shed more light in terms of deeper knowledge in this season.

> *Ephesians 1:9-10*
> *He made known to us the mystery of his will according to his good pleasure, which he purposed in Christ, to be put into effect when the times will have reached their fulfilment —to bring all things in heaven and on earth together under one head, even Christ.*

A new season has dawned called the fullness of the times. The Church needs to make necessary spiritual adjustments to comply with this season and its demands. God promised that when the times will have reached their fullness, He will bring all things both in heaven and on earth together in one under the headship of Jesus Christ. This means that everything under the sun is coming to a place of completeness or fullness. God wants the Church to enter into a new dimension called Jesus Christ. It is at this level we can experience the full measure of Christ and His anointing.

God, in this season, is releasing His anointing without measure upon the Church so that she can come to the full knowledge of His will through Jesus Christ. This season places a tremendous challenge upon the Church to come to a place of spiritual maturity in order to access her fullness and fulfilment in Christ.

There is a movement on the earth towards a place called oneness or unity. For Christ to be the Head of the Church on earth, the Church needs to start right away to destroy the walls of carnal division, man claimed doctrines and revelation that have for so long divided us. We need to embrace each other as Christians un-conditionally, to become one full functional body, for which Jesus Christ can be the head. Only in this fashion can the Church fully experience the leadership of Jesus Christ. We need to understand that Jesus Christ cannot be head over a Church with many scattered body members. All the members of the body must come together to be classifies as one body, the body of Jesus Christ.

John 10:10
The thief comes only to steal and kill and destroy;
I have come that they may have life, and have it to
the full.

Once again God is trying to reach out to mankind from a perspective of resourcefulness with life. God's plan has always been and will be to bless mankind with abundant life in its full measure. The word *life* covers all aspects of human activity including his health, ambitions, spiritual and earthly destinies, prosperity, finances resources, job, shelter, food, clothes, praise and worship capabilities, spiritual gifts and the dominion of his surrounding environment. Therefore when we have life it means we have all of the above and more.

God wants to resource us His Church with full life. It is only a matter of obedience that we can tap into this form of life. It is the same life Jesus Christ experienced whiles on the earth, revealing God's kingdom to the Church. Jesus lived a life full of God on earth; there was nothing in Him that was not of God, from His speech to His conduct. He became the visible form of the invisible God on earth.

> *Colossians 1:19*
> *For God was pleased to have all his fullness dwell in him, and through him to reconcile to himself all things, whether things on earth or things in heaven, by making peace through his blood, shed on the cross.*

Jesus' life-style was so conditioned and locked up in the purposes and the will of God that God became pleased with him. The word *pleased* also means to trust, in a deeper sense. God entrusted Jesus Christ with His very own fullness. Jesus Christ carried the deity of God in fullness whiles on the earth, establishing the kingdom of God. God still wants to do the same with His Church on earth, He wants His Church to carry the deity of His fullness at all times.

The season has come for the church to unleash her fullest potential to operate the last day signs and wonders. We need to encourage and activate the power of the Holy Spirit of God to take full control over our Church services and programs. Our programs are spiritually limiting and thereby compelling the Church to be religious.

The Church needs to break away from such religiously limiting mentalities in order to realize the full power of God in operation in these last days. Jesus Christ lived a pure, sinless and holy life whilst on earth, defying all works of satan and nailing them to the cross of Calvary. Christ fully executed all tasks entrusted to Him by God and kept all His command- ments. He lived to please God at all cost, regardless of the pressures and challenges he faced, resisting sin to the shedding of blood. Therefore God was pleased with Him and decided to have all fullness and the Godhead dwell in Him.

This season's challenge is to come to spiritual maturity so as to access fullness and fulfillment in Christ

The *fullness of God* also means divine heavenly back- up. Jesus Christ experienced a full heavenly back-up whilst on the earth. God had him fully protected and covered against all evil principalities and powers of darkness that could ever prevail against Him. When the Church walks in the fullness of God, He releases a heavenly back-up or a support system that ensures that whatever we do for God we have His cover till the work is completed. The Church needs to know that she is fully covered and divinely protected or immunized against the systems of darkness. Nothing can harm us for as long as we stay in and executing the will of God on the earth. This truth will help place the Church in a new dimension of God's fullness.

John 14:12
'He will do even greater things than these'

When Jesus Christ proclaimed such a statement he really meant it and knew that it will come to pass when the Church begins to walk in the season of God's fullness. There's no limitation in the fullness of God; nothing is impossible once we start walking in His fullness. Whatever is impossible in the natural realm suddenly becomes possible when we walk in the fullness of God. Surely the Church is able to do even greater things than those Jesus Christ had done. This is simply because of the limited time available to the End time Church. God is availing heavenly resources, pouring them out as rain upon His Church.

No eye has seen, no ear has heard, no mind has conceived what God has prepared for those who love Him (1 Corinthians 2:9). The church must consciously disconnect from religious slumber to fully embrace this scripture so that she is able to walk in His fullness and experience the full measure of Jesus Christ. When Jesus Christ said *greater*, I believe He also meant: with a 'greater momentum and acceleration;' with 'greater measure of faith;' with a 'greater anointing' with 'greater level to believe;' and with 'greater level of input and tenacity.' In this season, God has availed much more resources for the Church to perform and execute heavenly tasks on earth.

The Church must be more excited now than ever before, by simply realizing the measure of God's fullness poured upon her.

More supernatural signs and wonders

The fullness of the times is a dispensation whereby the Church is ushered in the dimension of doing supernatural exploits, as revealed in the book of Daniel. The Church has to be breaking a record of recorded supernatural exploits recorded in the Bible, she needs to out number them and make it her 21st century life-style. To see signs and wonders performed in the church services should become a norm and a habit for the Church. We should not be drawn to come in large numbers to see them performed over people.

Presently the opposite holds true in the Church. Where these miracles are visible, the more the people in the congregation. They come to verify for certain that it is God doing it through His servant(s). This is a great sign of disbelief from Christians towards God and may I say that God is totally displeased by such lack of faith and disbelief by the Church. After all, He has made all power available to us. The display of signs and wonders should become a Church life-style, such that we no longer focus on them, but on God rather, who must be worshiped in Spirit and in Truth. This weakness has caused the Church to resolve to the worship of the man of God than to worship the God of the man.

The drive must be on to normalize the miraculous signs and wonders, because they are merely a sign of God's display to the unsaved and unbelieving. The more connected and locked-up we are to God, the more God allows these signs to happen in our midst. The Church is power packed with all spiritual gifts, to help capacitate her to walk in the fullness of God.

More victories

The Church should perform a spiritual audit to ascertain the number of victories achieved through victorious and governmental prayers. There should be more spiritual as well as earthly victories achieved by the Church than there ever was in the Church's history. Considering the fact that God has made the glory of the latter Church greater than that of the former church; the present Church is more resourceful and heavenly empowered than the early Church. Therefore, she ought to manifest and bring forth more victories.

There needs to be a spiritual push to advance the Church to a place where there is more victories achieved. The last day Church must breakthrough to bring God more honour and glory. She must breakthrough till she puts all God's enemies under His footstool, because she has been granted such tremendous power. She is to demolish all strongholds and to make all the earthly kingdoms the kingdom of our God.

It is no doubt a lot of hard work, but fortunately God has already made things easy for the Church by blessing her with all spiritual blessings and gifts necessary to help accomplish the task. She just needs to trust and exercise her faith to a greater degree to realize her victories.

Jesus Christ is in no way coming back for a defeated Church or a bride with messy spots of bruises and sinfulness. He is rather coming back for a more victorious, powerful and a breakthrough Church. Jesus Christ fought all battles, for and on behalf of the Church, to deliver her to breakthrough point. All hard work has been done and accomplished in Jesus Christ.

More of God made manifest

There's an awesome responsibility resting upon the Church to fully manifest God on earth. This can be done through conversion of heathens to kingdom believers, display of healing miracles, proclamations, kingdom victories, and territorial and geographic land reclamations, economic and social victories. God wants to manifest Himself through every part of His earthly creation. All creation is duty bound to manifest the intents, purposes and the glory of God.

John 1:16
From the fullness of his grace we have all received one blessing after another.

The Church is receiving all earthly and heavenly gifts from the fullness of the grace which abided in Christ Jesus. God had to first fill His only son Jesus Christ with abundant grace. Subsequently the Church is receiving the same from Jesus Christ. The Church needs to first experience the fullness of the supply she needs through Jesus Christ before she can go out to minister to the demands of the worldly system.

> *Acts 2:4*
> *All of them were filled with the Holy Spirit and began to speak in other tongues as the Spirit enabled them.*

It is therefore very important that the Church waits upon God to fill her up with the power of His Holy Spirit, before embarking on the mission to go and heal and save the world. The Church can do nothing without the power of the Holy Spirit.

It is from this epicentre of grace, that the Church is able to download all spiritual and earthly relevant blessings. It is not by might or by power but by the grace of God. We are saved by the grace of God and not of our own works. When the Church receives blessings upon blessings it is still because of the abounding grace of God upon her.

Thus the impartation of spiritual gifts and calling are procured upon the Church from the fullness of Jesus Christ dimension. God allows all our needs to be met according to His glorious riches already downloaded in the person of Christ Jesus. The fullness of God or His deity remains the only and valid heavenly resources available to assist the Church accomplish her task in the earth.

Chapter 7

Unity of the Church

Unity of the Mind

Genesis 1:26
Then God said, "Let us make man in our image, in our likeness, and let them rule over the fish of the sea and the birds of the air, over the livestock, over all the earth, and over all creatures that move along the ground."

In the beginning when God created mankind He never did it alone, instead He said to His Godhead team, referring to the Jesus Christ and the Holy Spirit, let us make man in our own image, not in His individual image. We can see right from the beginning that God never worked alone. God is a good team player, in everything He does, He always engages people.

Amos 3:7
Surely the Sovereign Lord does nothing without revealing His plans to His servants the prophets.

Here we see that God never keeps anything crucial from His creation, He always engages them. God wants to engage His church; to work together as one unit, the body of Jesus Christ. We may be different members, but we all belong to the one body ultimately. Unity has long been a conceived idea in the mind of God. Jesus Christ came down to birth it, and the Church is the final product of this unity. Because God is united with Himself in the mind, hence we see it reflected in His plans and purposes.

All of God's creation is interdependent. Though a man was first created, then the woman from the man's rib, both should live united as one. When a man gets married he becomes one with his wife, for God never intended for him, the man, to live alone. All of creation, even animals, was created in two, a male and a female always. Again this portrays the status of unity.

2 Chronicles 30:12
Also in Judah the hand of God was on the people to give them unity of mind to carry out what the king and his officials had ordered, following the word of the Lord.

The mind has a crucial part to play in the facilitation of unity among God's people. The hand of God really played a crucial role in bringing deliverance to the mind-set of the people of Judah so that they could work together as one to accomplish what the word of the Lord had proclaimed. God knew that if they were not of one mind or sharing the same thinking patterns, they would have tremendous difficulty in accomplishing God's task.

He touched and delivered their scattered thinking patterns and brought them into oneness of mind. The biggest challenge of the Church in the 21st century is unity of the mind-set.

The main reason why so many different denominations emerge today is as a result of difference in terms of opinions and visions all of which are the product of the mind. The word of God says, *'as a man thinketh so is he (**Proverbs** 23:7-King James Authorised Version)*. We are the product of our own mind-sets.

Unity must first become the product of the mind, and then it will be translated into physical action. If the Church is not united in the mind, then she is bound to go in different directions and execute things differently and individually. The Church must embrace the fact that God's work is never for individuals, though individuals may have and operate in different gifts. However, all these gifts ought to work in harmony to produce one big task as ordained of the Lord.

> *Luke 9:1-4*
> *When Jesus had called out the Twelve together, he gave them power and authority to drive out all demons and to cure diseases, and he sent them out to preach the kingdom of God and to heal the sick. He told them: "Take nothing for the journey—no staff, no bag, no bread, no money, no extra tunic. Whatever house you enter, stay there until you leave that town.*

Jesus Christ could have sent out the twelve as individuals, however, he sent them out together as a group. This he did to teach them how God's Kingdom operated, how to value each others opinion, gifts; team work, to be a brother's keeper, and ultimately learn to work in unity. God never intends for us to live and operate in His Kingdom as separate individuals. Rather to always brings along someone to help us fulfil His vision and calling. This way we never get caught up in the 'my ministry syndrome' (my sheep, my tithes, my praise and worship, etc). The Kingdom of God is a united Kingdom. Those who operate and work in it, do so in the harmony of unity and not as individuals.

Unity in Worship

2 Kings 17:28-33

So one of the priests who had been exiled from Samaria came to live in Bethel and taught them how to worship the Lord.

Nevertheless, each national group made its own gods in the several towns where they settled, and set them up in the shrines the people of Samaria had made at the high places. The men from Babylon made Succoth Benoth, the men from Cuthah made Nergal, and the men from Hamath made Ashima, the Avvites made Nibhaz and Tartak, and the Shepharvites burned their children in the fire as sacrifices to Adrammelech and Anamelech, the gods of Sepharvaim.

They worshiped the Lord, but they also appointed all sorts of their own people to officiate for them as priests in the shrines at the high places. They worshiped the Lord, but they also served their own gods in accordance with the customs of the nations from which they had been brought.

The power and the strength of dissimilar vision and purpose are well displayed in this case study. Though the exiled priest came all the way from Samaria to Bethel and taught them how to worship God, nevertheless each national group conveniently made its own gods in several towns and worshiped them in high places.

When we worship God anyhow and differently than prescribed by Jesus Christ, God simply disqualifies and rejects such kind of worship

The Church of the 21st century is also caught up in a similar situation, although Jesus Christ came to show us the way to worship God. Nonetheless the Church is still divided in the opinion of worshiping God. Different churches have different styles and systems to worship God. Such disparity in worshipping God is based on the leader's ability to tune into the correct frequency and channel of what God has said to each leader before their appointment as shepherd; and what He is saying to them now.

The device of such systemic ways or worship was purely the product of the mind and individualistic architectural skills impression.

It never pleased God, purely because it was in defiance of the instruction as taught by the priest. Whenever we worship God, anyhow and differently than prescribed by Jesus Christ, God simply disqualifies and rejects such kind of worship.

A divided church cannot effectively worship God no matter how hard she can try. True worship comes out of unity of brotherhood, and as the Church corporately comes together to worship God. Nothing pleases God than seeing His church united in worship.

Unity of the Spirit
Romans 15:5
May the God who gives endurance and encouragement give you a spirit of unity among yourselves as you follow Christ Jesus, so that with one heart and mouth you may glorify the God and the Father of our Lord Jesus Christ.

Just as God is united with the Son and the Holy Spirit so should the Church brethren be with one another in spiritual unity. The Church often times forgets that her entire walk on the earth is a spiritual one. Therefore God requires of her to comply with spiritually related dynamics, including her unity in the spirit. Spiritual unity is the very power force of unity for the Church in the 21st century.

The Church must embrace the fact that her walk with Jesus Christ is a spiritual one, just as is her worship to God. Her totality of existence stems from the spiritual dimension. Therefore spiritual unity is one of the crucial forces that will help bring different parts of the body of Jesus Christ together, the Church.

As she becomes one in spirit so will she be in every other area of her existence. Spiritual unity must become the model for the 21st century Church's unity here on earth. The model of our earthly unity must be the same as that of the spiritual one. The Church needs to be a copy to reflect from whenever she talks about unity.

The winning formula for the Church is spiritual victory first then earthly manifestation. The Church cannot try to force earthly unity unless this has been accomplished in the spirit. Spiritual unity means having the same right attitude, faith, vision, heart, ambition and purpose to bring about and accomplish the same desired goals.

Romans 6:5
If we have been united with him like this in his death, we will certainly also be united with him in his resurrection.

Apostle Paul stresses the importance of spiritual unity in this passage of scripture. The Church needs to fully comprehend the fact that she was already united with Jesus Christ in His death.

When Jesus Christ died on the cross, the Church was already united with Him; hence she also died a spiritual death, and now awaits her eternal victory. When Christ Jesus was resurrected so was the Church. Hence she cannot face eternal condemnation. She has already conquered the devil by being locked up in the person Jesus Christ. Such unity with Christ Jesus brought forth eternal victory for the Church; the devil cannot believe his eyes. For, he had planned to annihilate Jesus Christ as an individual, thereby automatically defeating the Church. However, to his surprise the Church was already wrapped and locked up within Jesus Christ, who when He won, so did the Church within Him.

I think this is a very profound truth to embrace; subsequently Jesus Christ admires the fact that the Church has already overcome the devil. She is already seated with Him in the heavenly places (a place of eternal victory). This awesome yet much least proclaimed truth needs to become the moral fibre of the Church of the 21st century. Jesus Christ is expecting the Church to walk and remain sustained in this victory, till the Lord has made all kingdoms the kingdom of our God.

> *John 17:11, 20, 22, 23*
> *Holy Father, protect them by the power of your name—the name you gave me—so that they maybe one as we are one.*
>
> *My prayer is not for them alone. I pray also for those who will believe in me through their message, that all of them may be one. I have given them the glory you gave me, that they maybe one as we are one: I in them and you in me. May they be brought to complete unity to let the world know that you sent me and have loved them even as you have loved me.*

Unity of the Faith

> *Ephesians 4:11, 13*
> *It was he who gave some to be apostles, some to be prophets, some to be evangelists, and some to be pastors and teachers, to prepare God's people for works of service, so that the body of Christ may be built up until we all*

come to the unity of the faith and knowledge of the Son of God.

Philippians 2:5
Your attitude should be the same as that of Christ Jesus.

Christ believers need to embrace the same pattern and attitude as they work together to establish the Kingdom of God in the earth. The unity of attitude is very crucial as we strive to become the one body of Jesus Christ. Our attitudes should be the same towards one another, toward the work of God, toward the vision and purpose of building the Kingdom of God. Unity of attitude equals unity of the mind. The unity of the mind equals the unity of the entire body of Christ. The unity of attitude is therefore an interdependent element towards achieving the unity of whole body of believers in Christ.

Psalms 133:1
How good and pleasant it is when brothers live together in unity!

The psalmist David came under the anointing of the Spirit to write this scripture after carefully observing the brethren in his camp dwelling together in unity. It is very pleasant and a good thing to watch or experience in any given family fold. Let us bring this scripture home. There is nothing as pleasant and good as when all family members corporately, talk nicely to each other, exhorting and esteeming each other. There's that free flowing peace which overwhelms the mind, the body and the soul. It is everybody's desire to live under this kind of environment.

For a change, in David's camp, there was no fighting amongst the brethren; everything was flowing smoothly like the anointing flowing down Aaron's beard. This is a profound illustration David used. Let us look at it more in depth and find out what exactly David meant by it. The oil used to anoint kings and priests was very special, extracted from the olive leaves and carefully refined to achieve the desired effect. This kind of oil is a very thick substance, scented beautifully and used in the anointing process or occasion.

A beard is that hair that grows from under the chin, right up to the chicks of a male person. Some males grow it till it becomes very long, for recognition and they take pride in it and play with it.

When this smooth substance called oil is poured over the beard, which is a rough surface area, in the beginning there is resistance of flow. But with consistent pouring of the oil, the flowing begins and runs down smoothly through the beard till it reaches its tip. When unity prevails amongst brethren, you see what appears difficult to happen at first, then happening smoothly and harmoniously. And it becomes a beautiful thing to observe.

When brethren dwell together in unity, it is like a flow of musical sound, with each and every chord coming into harmony with the other. There is peace, stability, oneness, blessing and honour. God's purpose of creating mankind with different opinions, different race and colour suddenly is manifested, and can be enjoyed by all of His creation.